Scorpion Fish

Tori Miller

PowerKiDS
press

New York

Published in 2009 by The Rosen Publishing Group, Inc.
29 East 21st Street, New York, NY 10010

First Edition

Editor: Joanne Randolph
Book Design: Greg Tucker
Photo Researcher: Jessica Gerweck

Photo Credits: Cover, pp. 12–13, 15, 17, 19 Shutterstock.com; p. 5 © Ken Lucas/Getty Images; p. 7 © Brian J. Skerry/Getty Images; p. 9 © Dirscher/Reinhard/Age Fotostock; p. 11 © Ross Armstrong/Age Fotostock; p. 21 © Norbert Wu/Getty Images.

Library of Congress Cataloging-in-Publication Data

Miller, Tori.
  Scorpion fish / Tori Miller. — 1st ed.
     p. cm. — (Freaky fish)
  Includes index.
  ISBN 978-1-4358-2755-4 (library binding) — ISBN 978-1-4358-3172-8 (pbk.)
ISBN 978-1-4358-3178-0 (6-pack)
  1. Scorpionfishes—Juvenile literature. I. Title.
  QL638.S42M55 2009
  597'.68—dc22
                                                 2008032839

Manufactured in the United States of America

Contents

Is It a Rock or a Fish? 4

Big Heads, Poisonous Spines 6

At Home 8

A Quick Bite 10

The Scorpion Fish: Freaky Facts 12

A Look at the Lionfish 14

Poison! 16

Scorpion Fish Enemies 18

Scorpion Fish Babies 20

Poisonous Pets 22

Glossary 23

Index 24

Web Sites 24

Is It a Rock or a Fish?

Have you ever seen a scorpion fish? Perhaps you have, but you did not know it! Scorpion fish are very good at hiding in the places where they live. This is called **camouflage**. If there is a scorpion fish at the aquarium near you, you might need to look very carefully to see the fish. Scorpion fish are sometimes called rockfish because many **species** look like rocks!

There are 172 different species of scorpion fish. Scorpion fish can be many different sizes. The smallest ones are about the size of your pinky. The largest ones are about as long as you are!

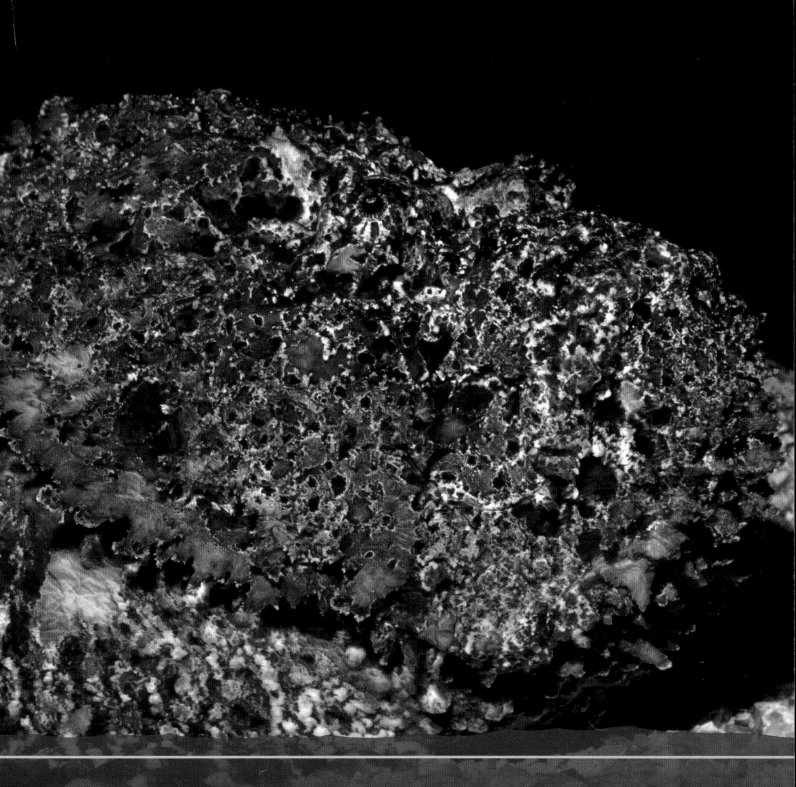

Can you see the scorpion fish in this photo? It is hard to see because it looks more like a rock than a fish!

Big Heads, Poisonous Spines

Scorpion fish have big heads and very big mouths! They also have bumpy bodies. Some species have folds and **frills** on their bodies, too. These bumps, folds, and frills make them look like rocks or seaweed. Scorpion fish also have coloring and markings that help them **blend** in.

Scorpion fish are not always big, but they are a danger to other fish and animals. Scorpion fish have sharp, **poisonous spines**. Most of the spines are along the middle of the scorpion fish's back. Scorpion fish may also have spines on their fins.

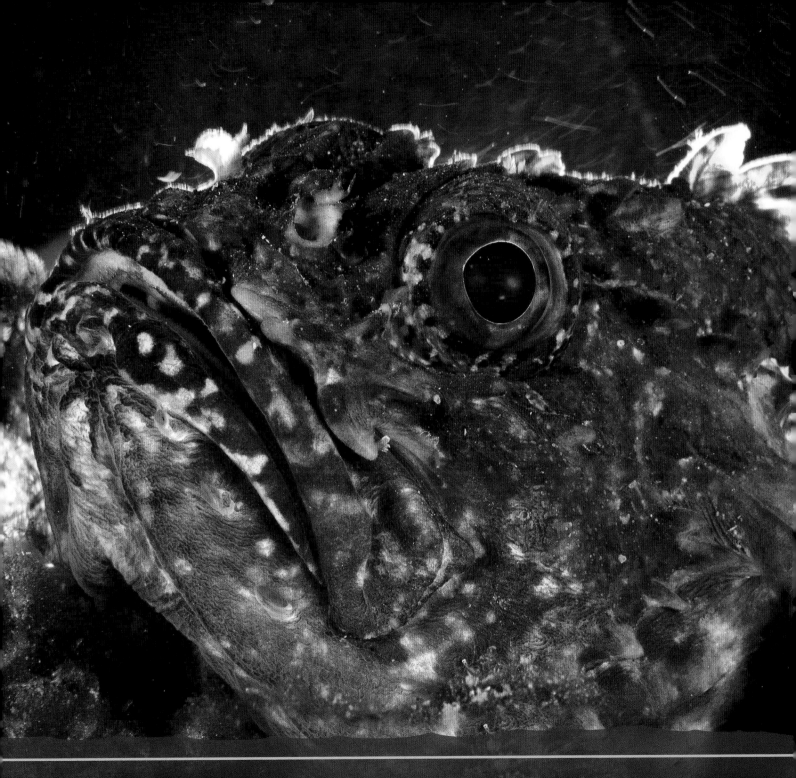

This scorpion fish has brown and green coloring and frills that help it blend in with seaweed. You can also see the big mouth for which scorpion fish are known.

Most scorpion fish live in the ocean, but a few species live in freshwater. Scorpion fish can be found in tropical and **temperate** waters around the world. There are large numbers of scorpion fish around Japan and near the Pacific coast of the United States.

Scorpion fish like shallow water, or water that is not deep. Scorpion fish live alone. They come together only to mate, or make babies. During the day, scorpion fish hide in caves, holes, or **coral reefs**. Some scorpion fish can cover themselves in the sand or mud. Scorpion fish hide all day and come out to hunt at night.

This lionfish has markings that help it blend in with the seaweed and coral reefs in the warm waters where it lives. Lionfish are also well liked as pets.

A Quick Bite

Scorpion fish eat other fish and crustaceans, which are animals with shells, such as shrimp and lobsters. Its unknowing **prey** likely never even sees the scorpion fish because it blends into its hiding place so well.

How does the scorpion fish do it? The scorpion fish is a master at waiting and watching. When a smaller fish gets close enough, the scorpion fish darts forward and snaps up the fish in its huge mouth. This all happens in under a second. If a person were watching, he or she would likely miss it!

When a scorpion fish, like this one, opens its mouth, the nearby prey gets sucked inside. As you can see, the mouth of the scorpion fish is quite large.

The Scorpion Fish:
Freaky Facts

- If you step on a scorpion fish, the best way to treat the wound made by its spines is to run it under hot water as soon as possible. The hot water breaks down the poison.

- A scorpion fish can swallow prey that is up to half the size of its own body!

- **Algae** grow on some kinds of scorpion fish. This makes them look even more like rocks!

- Most scorpion fish can shed their skin.

- One kind of scorpion fish, called the stonefish, sometimes hunts by trapping its prey near rocks or coral reefs.

∘Unlike other kinds of scorpion fish, the stonefish will sometimes jab its spines at enemies.

∘The pygmy scorpion fish is only about 1.5 inches (4 cm) long.

∘The leaf scorpion fish fools its prey by looking almost exactly like a leaf. It even drifts in the water like a leaf.

A Look at the Lionfish

Not all scorpion fish hide among the rocks. The brightly striped lionfish has a different way of hunting. The body of a lionfish is only about 1 foot (30 cm) long, but it can look much bigger because it has long spines. These long spines and the fish's bright stripes make it look like floating seaweed. The lionfish uses this to its advantage as it hunts.

When it sees a yummy fish, the lionfish swims slowly toward its prey. The smaller fish does not know it is in danger. Suddenly, it is sucked into the lionfish's huge mouth!

Some lionfish have black and white stripes like a zebra. Others have yellow, orange, or red stripes, as this one does.

Poison!

Scorpion fish are some of the most poisonous fish in the world! For example, a kind of scorpion fish called the stonefish is thought to be the deadliest fish in the world. The spines of the stonefish, like other scorpion fish, have dents in them. The poison runs through the dents and into the wound made by the spine. People have been hurt or even killed by stepping on scorpion fish that are resting on the ocean floor.

Scorpion fish do not use their spines to catch prey. They use their spines only to keep themselves safe from **predators**.

Stonefish get their name because they look like an algae-covered rock, as does this one. Prey swimming nearby do not see the stonefish lying in wait until it is too late.

Scorpion Fish Enemies

Adult scorpion fish are not preyed upon often because of their poisonous spines. Many species of scorpion fish have bright colors that warn other fish to stay away. However, large fish or sea lions may eat young scorpion fish.

The scorpion fish's biggest predators are people. Although the spines of the scorpion fish are poisonous, the flesh is not. Many people like to eat the larger species of scorpion fish. In Hong Kong, stonefish are often sold alive at the markets. People who buy these fish must be very careful! Have you ever eaten a scorpion fish?

This scorpion fish is brightly colored to let predators know it tastes bad. It also has frills and markings that

Scorpion Fish Babies

Most kinds of scorpion fish do not lay eggs. Instead, they give birth to live young. Baby scorpion fish are called **larvae**. A scorpion fish can give birth to thousands of larvae at one time. Larvae grow into juvenile, or young, scorpion fish and then they become adults.

One type of scorpion fish that does lay eggs is the California scorpion fish. A California scorpion fish lays her eggs in two pear-shaped balloons. These balloons float to the top of the water. When the larvae break free from the egg, they fall to the bottom of the ocean.

This is a juvenile lionfish, which likely spent up to 40 days as a tiny larva. As the fish grows, its markings will become darker.

Poisonous Pets

People like to look at some scorpion fish because of their bright colors and long spines. You can often see scorpion fish at a public aquarium. Some people keep scorpion fish in home aquariums, too.

People who keep scorpion fish need to take good care of them. Scorpion fish must live alone because they will eat almost any other fish that shares their home. People who keep scorpion fish must also be careful not to touch the fish's spines. These pet owners do not seem to mind doing these things, though. They love to watch this freaky fish!

algae (AL-jee) Plantlike living things without roots or stems that live in water.

blend (BLEND) To match what is around something.

camouflage (KA-muh-flahj) A color or shape that matches what is around something and helps hide it.

coral reefs (KOR-ul REEFS) Underwater hills of coral, or hard matter made up of the bones of tiny sea animals.

frills (FRILZ) Decorations or small, fancy parts.

larvae (LAHR-vee) Bugs or fish in the early life stage in which they have a wormlike form.

poisonous (POYZ-nus) Causing pain or death.

predators (PREH-duh-terz) Animals that kill other animals for food.

prey (PRAY) An animal that is hunted by another animal for food.

species (SPEE-sheez) One kind of living thing. All people are one species.

spines (SPYNZ) Sharp, pointy things.

temperate (TEM-puh-rut) Not too hot or too cold.

Index

A
aquarium, 4, 22

B
bodies, 6, 12, 14

C
coral reefs, 8, 12

D
danger, 6, 14

F
freshwater, 8

L
larvae, 20

M
markings, 6
middle, 6
mouth(s), 6, 10, 14

O
ocean, 8, 20

P
pinky, 4
place, 4, 10
predators, 16, 18
prey, 10, 12, 14, 16

R
rockfish, 4
rocks, 4, 6, 12, 14

S
seaweed, 6, 14
size(s), 4, 12
species, 4, 6, 8, 18
spines, 6, 12–14, 16, 18, 22

W
water(s), 8, 12–13, 20
world, 8, 16

Web Sites

Due to the changing nature of Internet links, PowerKids Press has developed an online list of Web sites related to the subject of this book. This site is updated regularly. Please use this link to access the list:

www.powerkidslinks.com/ffish/scorpion/